pause & reflect

MEDITATIONS FOR COMMUNITY

pause & reflect

MEDITATIONS FOR COMMUNITY

ONE VOICE
PRESS

WILMETTE, ILLINOIS

One Voice Press
1233 Central St., Evanston, IL 60202

Printed in the United States of America on
acid-free paper ∞

ISBN: 978-1-61851-221-5
25   24   23   22   4   3   2   1

Cover design by Carlos Esparza
Book design by Patrick Falso

CONTENTS

INTRODUCTION

There is much in our modern world compet-
ing for our attention. Technology is changing
at a pace so rapid that most of us cannot keep
up, let alone take the time to process the ways
in which it is affecting us. As we go about our
daily lives we are seemingly assaulted with
an endless series of distractions. The need to
retreat from the stress and chaos that so often
surrounds us, to center ourselves and reflect on
our inner reality, has never been of more vital
importance. It is with this in mind that One
Voice Press is happy to present this, the fourth
title in its *Pause & Reflect* series.

Pause & Reflect is a series that presents med-
itative passages from the writings of the Bahá'í
Faith arranged around particular themes.
While the Bahá'í Faith places a great deal of
importance on meditation and the cultivation
of spirituality, it is also a religion that calls for

action and societal transformation. Meditation, from a Bahá'í perspective, is not exclusively a means for personal growth but also a tool that should equip us with insights and awareness that can be translated into action in our lives and in the communities in which we live.

This brings us to the theme of this book: Community. As human beings, we are not meant to live in isolation, but rather to be part of communities. Our relationships and collaborations with others are vital aspects of our existence and our ability to thrive. A community with a shared sense of purpose is a powerful thing, and when that shared sense of purpose is rooted in the desire to contribute to the betterment of society, then a community has the potential for transformative change. This notion is at the heart of Bahá'í-inspired community building efforts all over the world.

In every corner of the globe, in settings both rural and urban, Bahá'ís are working to build vibrant communities based on principles such as justice, equality, and the oneness of the human family. Weaving together worship and practical actions for the promotion of the common good, these efforts are open to all who wish to participate. The goal of these initiatives, inspired by the principles and teachings of the Faith, is to raise the capacity of people to take charge of their own spiritual, social, and intellectual growth and become active agents in their own development, as well as that of their communities.

The quotations collected in this volume are just a small sampling of the wealth of material that the Bahá'í writings offer on the subject. It is hoped that readers will draw insight from these pages, and be inspired to explore the subject further.

Unity & Cooperation

BAHÁ'U'LLÁH

1

We love to see you at all times consorting in amity and concord within the paradise of My good-pleasure, and to inhale from your acts the fragrance of friendliness and unity, of loving-kindness and fellowship. Thus counseleth you the All-Knowing, the Faithful. We shall always be with you; if We inhale the perfume of your fellowship, Our heart will assuredly rejoice, for naught else can satisfy Us.

2

Cleave unto that which draweth you together and uniteth you. This, verily, is the most exalted Word which the Mother Book hath sent down and revealed unto you.

3

It behooveth man to adhere tenaciously unto that which will promote fellowship, kindliness and unity.

4

He Who is your Lord, the All-Merciful, cherisheth in His heart the desire of beholding the entire human race as one soul and one body.

5

The utterance of God is a lamp, whose light is these words: Ye are the fruits of one tree, and the leaves of one branch. Deal ye one with another with the utmost love and harmony, with friendliness and fellowship. He Who is the Daystar of Truth beareth Me witness! So powerful is the light of unity that it can illuminate the whole earth. The One true God, He Who knoweth all things, Himself testifieth to the truth of these words.

Exert yourselves that ye may attain this transcendent and most sublime station, the station that can insure the protection and security of all mankind. This goal excelleth every other goal, and this aspiration is the monarch of all aspirations.

6

O Children of Men! Know ye not why We created you all from the same dust? That no one should exalt himself over the other. Ponder at all times in your hearts how ye were created. Since We have created you all from one same substance it is incumbent on you to be even as one soul, to walk with the same feet, eat with the same mouth and dwell in the same land, that from your inmost being, by your deeds and actions, the signs of oneness and the essence of detachment may be made manifest. Such is My counsel to you, O concourse of light! Heed ye this counsel that ye may obtain the fruit of holiness from the tree of wondrous glory.

'ABDU'L-BAHÁ

7

The supreme need of humanity is cooperation and reciprocity. The stronger the ties of fellowship and solidarity amongst men, the greater will be the power of constructiveness and accomplishment in all the planes of human activity. Without cooperation and reciprocal attitude the individual member of human society remains self-centered, uninspired by altruistic purposes, limited and solitary in development like the animal and plant organisms of the lower kingdoms.

8

When you love a member of your family or a compatriot, let it be with a ray of the Infinite Love! Let it be in God, and for God! Wherever you find the attributes of God love that person, whether he be of your family or of another. Shed the light of a boundless love on every human being whom you meet, whether of your country, your race, your political party, or of any other nation, color or shade of political opinion. Heaven will support you while you work in this ingathering of the scattered peoples of the world beneath the shadow of the almighty tent of unity.

9

Be in perfect unity. Never become angry with one another. . . . Love the creatures for the sake of God and not for themselves. You will never become angry or impatient if you love them for the sake of God. Humanity is not perfect. There are imperfections in every human being, and you will always become unhappy if you look toward the people themselves. But if you look toward God, you will love them and be kind to them, for the world of God is the world of perfection and complete mercy.

10

In cycles gone by, though harmony was established, yet, owing to the absence of means, the unity of all mankind could not have been achieved. Continents remained widely divided, nay even among the peoples of one and the same continent association and interchange of thought were well-nigh impossible. Consequently intercourse, understanding and unity amongst all the peoples and kindreds of the earth were unattainable. In this day, however, means of communication have multiplied, and the five continents of the earth have virtually merged into one. And for everyone it is now easy to travel to any land, to associate and exchange views with its peoples, and to become familiar, through publications, with the conditions, the religious beliefs and the thoughts of all men. In like manner all the members of the human family, whether peoples or governments, cities or villages, have become increasingly interdependent. For none is self-sufficiency any longer possible, inasmuch as political ties unite all peoples and nations, and the bonds of trade and industry, of agriculture and education, are being strengthened every day. Hence the unity of all mankind can in this day be achieved.

11

O ye loved ones of the Lord! This is the hour when ye must associate with all the earth's peoples in extreme kindliness and love, and be to them the signs and tokens of God's great mercy. Ye must become the very soul of the world . . .

12

Let them purify their sight and behold all humankind as leaves and blossoms and fruits of the tree of being. Let them at all times concern themselves with doing a kindly thing for one of their fellows, offering to someone love, consideration, thoughtful help. Let them see no one as their enemy, or as wishing them ill, but think of all humankind as their friends . . .

13

Wherefore must the loved ones of God associate in affectionate fellowship with stranger and friend alike, showing forth to all the utmost loving-kindness, disregarding the degree of their capacity, never asking whether they deserve to be loved. In every instance let the friends be considerate and infinitely kind.

14

The great and fundamental teachings of Bahá'u'lláh are the oneness of God and unity of mankind. This is the bond of union among Bahá'ís all over the world. They become united among themselves, then unite others. It is impossible to unite unless united. Christ said, "Ye are the salt of the earth; but if the salt has lost his savor, wherewith shall it be salted?" This proves there were dissensions and lack of unity among His followers. Hence His admonition to unity of action.

Now must we, likewise, bind ourselves together in the utmost unity, be kind and loving to each other, sacrificing all our possessions, our honor, yea, even our lives for each other. Then will it be proved that we have acted according to the teachings of God, that we have been real believers in the oneness of God and unity of mankind.

15

A t a time when warfare and strife prevailed among nations, when enmity and hatred separated sects and denominations and human differences were very great, Bahá'u'lláh appeared upon the horizon of the East, proclaiming the oneness of God and the unity of the world of humanity. He promulgated the teaching that all mankind are the servants of one God; that all have come into being through the bestowal of the one Creator; that God is kind to all, nurtures, rears and protects all, provides for all and extends His love and mercy to all races and people. Inasmuch as God is loving, why should we be unjust and unkind? As God manifests loyalty and mercy, why should we show forth enmity and hatred? Surely the divine policy is more perfect than human plan and theory; for no matter how wise and sagacious man may become, he can never attain a policy that is superior to the policy of God. Therefore, we must emulate the attitude of God, love all people, be just and kind to every human creature.

SHOGHI EFFENDI

16

Unification of the whole of mankind is the hall-mark of the stage which human society is now approaching. Unity of family, of tribe, of city-state, and nation have been successively attempted and fully established. World unity is the goal towards which a harassed humanity is striving.

17

God's purpose is none other than to usher in, in ways He alone can bring about, and the full significance of which He alone can fathom, the Great, the Golden Age of a long-divided, a long-afflicted humanity. Its present state, indeed even its immediate future, is dark, distressingly dark. Its distant future, however, is radiant, gloriously radiant—so radiant that no eye can visualize it.

18

Most important of all is that love and unity should prevail in the Bahá'í Community, as this is what people are most longing for in the present dark state of the world. Words without the living example will never be sufficient to breathe hope into the hearts of a disillusioned and often cynical generation.

THE UNIVERSAL HOUSE
OF JUSTICE

19

. . . the friends must guard against being drawn into the ultimately futile conflict and strife that characterizes so much of the discussion of the affairs of society, or—heaven forbid—allowing interaction of this type to permeate, even fleetingly, the conversations of the community. Yet such vigilance on your part in avoiding discord and in not becoming entangled in society's controversies should under no circumstances be construed as aloofness from the many pressing concerns of this time. Far from it. You are among the most active and earnest of humanity's well-wishers. But, whether through deeds or words, the merit of your every contribution to social well-being lies, first, in your resolute commitment to discover that precious point of unity where contrasting perspectives overlap and around which contending peoples can coalesce.

20

. . . the principle that is to infuse all facets of organized life on the planet is the oneness of humankind, the hallmark of the age of maturity. That humanity constitutes a single people is a truth that, once viewed with skepticism, claims widespread acceptance today. The rejection of deeply ingrained prejudices and a growing sense of world citizenship are among the signs of this heightened awareness. Yet, however promising the rise in collective consciousness may be, it should be seen as only the first step of a process that will take decades—nay, centuries—to unfold. For the principle of the oneness of humankind, as proclaimed by Bahá'u'lláh, asks not merely for cooperation among people and nations. It calls for a complete reconceptualization of the relationships that sustain society.

Consultation, Action, Reflection, and Study

BAHÁ'U'LLÁH

1

Take ye counsel together in all matters, inasmuch as consultation is the lamp of guidance which leadeth the way, and is the bestower of understanding.

2

Consultation bestoweth greater awareness and transmuteth conjecture into certitude. It is a shining light which, in a dark world, leadeth the way and guideth. For everything there is and will continue to be a station of perfection and maturity. The maturity of the gift of understanding is made manifest through consultation.

3

The Great Being saith: The heaven of divine wisdom is illumined with the two luminaries of consultation and compassion. Take ye counsel together in all matters, inasmuch as consultation is the lamp of guidance which leadeth the way, and is the bestower of understanding.

4

Say: no man can attain his true station except through his justice. No power can exist except through unity. No welfare and no well-being can be attained except through consultation.

5

In all things it is necessary to consult. This matter should be forcibly stressed by thee, so that consultation may be observed by all. The intent of what hath been revealed from the Pen of the Most High is that consultation may be fully carried out among the friends, inasmuch as it is and will always be a cause of awareness and of awakening and a source of good and well-being.

'ABDU'L-BAHÁ

6

The question of consultation is of the utmost importance, and is one of the most potent instruments conducive to the tranquillity and felicity of the people. For example, when a believer is uncertain about his affairs, or when he seeketh to pursue a project or trade, the friends should gather together and devise a solution for him. He, in his turn, should act accordingly. Likewise in larger issues, when a problem ariseth, or a difficulty occurreth, the wise should gather, consult, and devise a solution. They should then rely upon the one true God, and surrender to His Providence, in whatever way it may be revealed, for divine confirmations will undoubtedly assist. Consultation, therefore, is one of the explicit ordinances of the Lord of mankind.

7

Man must consult on all matters, whether major or minor, so that he may become cognizant of what is good. Consultation giveth him insight into things and enableth him to delve into questions which are unknown. The light of truth shineth from the faces of those who engage in consultation. Such consultation causeth the living waters to flow in the meadows of man's reality, the rays of ancient glory to shine upon him, and the tree of his being to be adorned with wondrous fruit. The members who are consulting, however, should behave in the utmost love, harmony and sincerity towards each other. The principle of consultation is one of the most fundamental elements of the divine edifice. Even in their ordinary affairs the individual members of society should consult.

8

Settle all things, both great and small, by consultation. Without prior consultation, take no important step in your own personal affairs. Concern yourselves with one another. Help along one another's projects and plans. Grieve over one another. Let none in the whole country go in need. Befriend one another until ye become as a single body, one and all . . .

9

The prime requisites for them that take counsel together are purity of motive, radiance of spirit, detachment from all else save God, attraction to His Divine Fragrances, humility and lowliness amongst His loved ones, patience and long-suffering in difficulties and servitude to His exalted Threshold. Should they be graciously aided to acquire these attributes, victory from the unseen Kingdom of Bahá shall be vouchsafed to them.

10

The members thereof must take counsel together in such wise that no occasion for ill-feeling or discord may arise. This can be attained when every member expresseth with absolute freedom his own opinion and setteth forth his argument. Should any one oppose, he must on no account feel hurt for not until matters are fully discussed can the right way be revealed. The shining spark of truth cometh forth only after the clash of differing opinions. If after discussion a decision be carried unanimously, well and good; but if, the Lord forbid, differences of opinion should arise, a majority of voices must prevail.

11

In this Cause consultation is of vital importance, but spiritual conference and not the mere voicing of personal views is intended. . . .

The purpose is to emphasize the statement that consultation must have for its object the investigation of truth. He who expresses an opinion should not voice it as correct and right but set it forth as a contribution to the consensus of opinion, for the light of reality becomes apparent when two opinions coincide. A spark is produced when flint and steel come together. Man should weigh his opinions with the utmost serenity, calmness and composure. Before expressing his own views he should carefully consider the views already advanced by others. If he finds that a previously expressed opinion is more true and worthy, he should accept it immediately and not willfully hold to an opinion of his own. By this excellent method he endeavors to arrive at unity and truth. Opposition and division are deplorable. . . . Love and fellowship are the foundation.

12

If a small number of people gather lovingly together, with absolute purity and sanctity, with their hearts free of the world, experiencing the emotions of the Kingdom and the powerful magnetic forces of the Divine, and being at one in their happy fellowship, that gathering will exert its influence over all the earth. The nature of that band of people, the words they speak, the deeds they do, will unleash the bestowals of Heaven, and provide a foretaste of eternal bliss. The hosts of the Company on high will defend them, and the angels of the Abhá Paradise, in continuous succession, will come down to their aid.

13

The purpose of consultation is to show that the views of several individuals are assuredly preferable to one man, even as the power of a number of men is of course greater than the power of one man. Thus consultation is acceptable in the presence of the Almighty, and hath been enjoined upon the believers, so that they may confer upon ordinary and personal matters, as well as on affairs which are general in nature and universal.

13

SHOGHI EFFENDI

14

Let us also bear in mind that the keynote of the Cause of God is not dictatorial authority but humble fellowship, not arbitrary power, but the spirit of frank and loving consultation. Nothing short of the spirit of a true Bahá'í can hope to reconcile the principles of mercy and justice, of freedom and submission, of the sanctity of the right of the individual and of self-surrender, of vigilance, discretion and prudence on the one hand, and fellowship, candor, and courage on the other.

15

Not infrequently, nay oftentimes, the most lowly, untutored and inexperienced among the friends [Bahá'ís] will, by the sheer inspiring force of selfless and ardent devotion, contribute a distinct and memorable share to a highly involved discussion in any given Assembly.

16

The principle of consultation, which constitutes one of the basic laws of the Administration, should be applied to all Bahá'í activities which affect the collective interests of the Faith, for it is through co-operation and continual exchange of thoughts and views that the Cause can best safeguard and foster its interests. Individual initiative, personal ability and resourcefulness, though indispensable, are, unless supported and enriched by the collective experiences and wisdom of the group, utterly incapable of achieving such a tremendous task.

17

The Bahá'ís must learn to forget personalities and to overcome the desire—so natural in people—to take sides and fight about it. They must also learn to really make use of the great principle of consultation.

THE UNIVERSAL HOUSE
OF JUSTICE

18

Thousands upon thousands, embracing the diversity of the entire human family, are engaged in systematic study of the Creative Word in an environment that is at once serious and uplifting. As they strive to apply through a process of action, reflection and consultation the insights thus gained, they see their capacity to serve the Cause rise to new levels. Responding to the inmost longing of every heart to commune with its Maker, they carry out acts of collective worship in diverse settings, uniting with others in prayer, awakening spiritual susceptibilities, and shaping a pattern of life distinguished for its devotional character.

19

As a person cultivates the habit of study and deep reflection upon the Creative Word, this process of transformation reveals itself in an ability to express one's understanding of profound concepts and to explore spiritual reality in conversations of significance. These capacities are visible not only in the elevated discussions that increasingly characterize interactions within the community, but in the ongoing conversations that reach well beyond. . . . Through exchanges of this kind, consciousness of spiritual forces is raised, apparent dichotomies yield to unexpected insights, a sense of unity and common calling is fortified, confidence that a better world can be created is strengthened, and a commitment to action becomes manifest.

20

It is not possible for you to effect the transformation envisioned by Bahá'u'lláh merely by adopting the perspectives, practices, concepts, criticisms, and language of contemporary society. Your approach, instead, will be distinguished by maintaining a humble posture of learning, weighing alternatives in the light of His teachings, consulting to harmonize differing views and shape collective action, and marching forward with unbreakable unity in serried lines.

21

Numerous, of course, are the questions that the process of learning, now under way in all regions of the world, must address: how to bring people of different backgrounds together in an environment which, devoid of the constant threat of conflict and distinguished by its devotional character, encourages them to put aside the divisive ways of a partisan mindset, fosters higher degrees of unity of thought and action, and elicits wholehearted participation . . . To explore questions such as these and the many others certain to arise, the Bahá'í community has adopted a mode of operation characterized by action, reflection, consultation and study—study which involves not only constant reference to the writings of the Faith but also the scientific analysis of patterns unfolding. Indeed, how to maintain such a mode of learning in action, how to ensure that growing numbers participate in the generation and application of relevant knowledge, and how to devise structures for the systemization of an expanding worldwide experience and for the equitable distribution of the lessons learned—these are, themselves, the object of regular examination.

22

In more and more clusters, the programme of growth is increasing in scope and complexity, commensurate with the rising capacity of the [Divine] Plan's three protagonists—the individual, the community, and the institutions of the Faith—to create a mutually supportive environment. And we are delighted that, as anticipated, there are a growing number of clusters where a hundred or more individuals are now facilitating the engagement of a thousand or more in weaving a pattern of life, spiritual, dynamic, transformative. Underlying the process even from the start is, of course, a collective movement towards the vision of material and spiritual prosperity set forth by Him Who is the Lifegiver of the World. But when such large numbers are involved, the movement of an entire population becomes discernible.

Elimination of
Prejudices

BAHÁ'U'LLÁH

1

Illumine and hallow your hearts; let them not be profaned by the thorns of hate or the thistles of malice. Ye dwell in one world, and have been created through the operation of one Will. Blessed is he who mingleth with all men in a spirit of utmost kindliness and love.

2

Exalted, immensely exalted is He Who hath removed differences and established harmony. Glorified, infinitely glorified is He Who hath caused discord to cease, and decreed solidarity and unity. Praised be God, the Pen of the Most High hath lifted distinctions from between His servants and handmaidens, and, through His consummate favours and all-encompassing mercy, hath conferred upon all a station and rank of the same plane. He hath broken the back of vain imaginings with the sword of utterance and hath obliterated the perils of idle fancies through the pervasive power of His might.

3

O ye that dwell on earth! The distinguishing feature that marketh the preeminent character of this Supreme Revelation consisteth in that We have, on the one hand, blotted out from the pages of God's holy Book whatsoever hath been the cause of strife, of malice and mischief amongst the children of men, and have, on the other, laid down the essential prerequisites of concord, of understanding, of complete and enduring unity. Well is it with them that keep My statutes.

'ABDU'L-BAHÁ

4

A fundamental teaching of Bahá'u'lláh is the oneness of the world of humanity. Addressing mankind, He says, "Ye are all leaves of one tree and the fruits of one branch." By this it is meant that the world of humanity is like a tree, the nations or peoples are the different limbs or branches of that tree, and the individual human creatures are as the fruits and blossoms thereof. In this way Bahá'u'lláh expressed the oneness of humankind, whereas in all religious teachings of the past the human world has been represented as divided into two parts: one known as the people of the Book of God, or the pure tree, and the other the people of infidelity and error, or the evil tree. The former were considered as belonging to the faithful, and the others to the hosts of the irreligious and infidel—one part of humanity the recipients of divine mercy, and the other the object of the wrath of their Creator. Bahá'u'lláh removed this by proclaiming the oneness of the world of humanity. . . .

5

And the breeding ground of all these tragedies is prejudice: prejudice of race and nation, of religion, of political opinion; and the root cause of prejudice is blind imitation of the past—imitation in religion, in racial attitudes, in national bias, in politics. So long as this aping of the past persisteth, just so long will the foundations of the social order be blown to the four winds, just so long will humanity be continually exposed to direst peril.

6

But there is need of a superior power to overcome human prejudices, a power which nothing in the world of mankind can withstand and which will overshadow the effect of all other forces at work in human conditions. That irresistible power is the love of God. It is my hope and prayer that it may destroy the prejudice of this one point of distinction between you and unite you all permanently under its hallowed protection.

7

It is evident that prejudices arising from adherence to religious forms and imitation of ancestral beliefs have hindered the progress of humanity thousands of years. How many wars and battles have been fought, how much division, discord and hatred have been caused by this form of prejudice!

8

Prejudices of all kinds—whether religious, racial, patriotic or political—are destructive of divine foundations in man. All the warfare and bloodshed in human history have been the outcome of prejudice. This earth is one home and native land. God has created mankind with equal endowment and right to live upon the earth. As a city is the home of all its inhabitants although each may have his individual place of residence therein, so the earth's surface is one wide native land or home for all races of humankind. Racial prejudice or separation into nations such as French, German, American and so on is unnatural and proceeds from human motive and ignorance. All are the children and servants of God. Why should we be separated by artificial and imaginary boundaries? In the animal kingdom the doves flock together in harmony and agreement. They have no prejudices. We are human and superior in intelligence. Is it befitting that lower creatures should manifest virtues which lack expression in man?

9

Prejudices of religion, race or sect destroy the foundation of humanity.

All the divisions in the world, hatred, war and bloodshed, are caused by one or other of these prejudices.

The whole world must be looked upon as one single country, all the nations as one nation, all men as belonging to one race. Religions, races, and nations are all divisions of man's making only, and are necessary only in his thought; before God there are neither Persians, Arabs, French nor English; God is God for all, and to Him all creation is one. We must obey God, and strive to follow Him by leaving all our prejudices and bringing about peace on earth.

10

In order to find truth we must give up our prejudices, our own small trivial notions; an open receptive mind is essential. If our chalice is full of self, there is no room in it for the water of life. The fact that we imagine ourselves to be right and everybody else wrong is the greatest of all obstacles in the path towards unity, and unity is necessary if we would reach truth, for truth is *one*.

Therefore it is imperative that we should renounce our own particular prejudices and superstitions if we earnestly desire to seek the truth. Unless we make a distinction in our minds between dogma, superstition and prejudice on the one hand, and truth on the other, we cannot succeed. When we are in earnest in our search for anything we look for it everywhere. This principle we must carry out in our search for truth.

11

In this day man must investigate reality impartially and without prejudice in order to reach the true knowledge and conclusions. What, then, constitutes the inequality between man and woman? Both are human. In powers and function each is the complement of the other. At most it is this: that woman has been denied the opportunities which man has so long enjoyed, especially the privilege of education.

12

And among the teachings of Bahá'u'lláh is the equality of women and men. The world of humanity has two wings—one is women and the other men. Not until both wings are equally developed can the bird fly. Should one wing remain weak, flight is impossible. Not until the world of women becomes equal to the world of men in the acquisition of virtues and perfections, can success and prosperity be attained as they ought to be.

13

. . . until woman and man recognize and realize equality, social and political progress here or anywhere will not be possible. For the world of humanity consists of two parts or members: one is woman; the other is man. Until these two members are equal in strength, the oneness of humanity cannot be established, and the happiness and felicity of mankind will not be a reality. God willing, this is to be so.

SHOGHI EFFENDI

14

. . . interracial fellowship completely purged from the curse of racial prejudice which stigmatizes the vast majority of its people—these are the weapons which the American believers can and must wield in their double crusade, first to regenerate the inward life of their own community, and next to assail the long-standing evils that have entrenched themselves in the life of their nation.

15

It is difficult for the friends always to remember that in matter[s] where race enters, a hundred times more consideration and wisdom in handling situations is necessary than when an issue is not complicated by this factor.

16

As to racial prejudice, the corrosion of which, for well-nigh a century, has bitten into the fiber, and attacked the whole social structure of American society, it should be regarded as constituting the most vital and challenging issue confronting the Bahá'í community at the present stage of its evolution. The ceaseless exertions which this issue of paramount importance calls for, the sacrifices it must impose, the care and vigilance it demands, the moral courage and fortitude it requires, the tact and sympathy it necessitates, invest this problem, which the American believers are still far from having satisfactorily resolved, with an urgency and importance that cannot be overestimated.

THE UNIVERSAL HOUSE
OF JUSTICE

17

Racism is a profound deviation from the standard of true morality. It deprives a portion of humanity of the opportunity to cultivate and express the full range of their capability and to live a meaningful and flourishing life, while blighting the progress of the rest of humankind. It cannot be rooted out by contest and conflict. It must be supplanted by the establishment of just relationships among individuals, communities, and institutions of society that will uplift all and will not designate anyone as "other." The change required is not merely social and economic, but above all moral and spiritual.

18

The problems related to class prejudice which you have experienced and observed are noted, and the suggestions you offer for working toward their remedy are truly appreciated. As you know, the Bahá'ís are distinguished not by their perfection or their immunity from the negative influences of the wider society in which they live, but by their acceptance of Bahá'u'lláh's vision and willingness to work toward it. Each of us must strike a balance between realistically facing our community's shortcomings, and focusing on Bahá'u'lláh's Teachings rather than our fellow believers as our standard of faith. This comment is not intended to belittle your concerns, but rather to place them in perspective so that you may not become discouraged as you strive toward the ideal.

19

The primary question to be resolved is how the present world, with its entrenched pattern of conflict, can change to a world in which harmony and cooperation will prevail.

World order can be founded only on an unshakable consciousness of the oneness of mankind, a spiritual truth which all the human sciences confirm. Anthropology, physiology, psychology, recognize only one human species, albeit infinitely varied in the secondary aspects of life. Recognition of this truth requires abandonment of prejudice—prejudice of every kind—race, class, color, creed, nation, sex, degree of material civilization, everything which enables people to consider themselves superior to others.

Acceptance of the oneness of mankind is the first fundamental prerequisite for reorganization and administration of the world as one country, the home of humankind. Universal acceptance of this spiritual principle is essential to any successful attempt to establish world peace.

20

. . . there are certain fundamental concepts that all should bear in mind. One is the centrality of knowledge to social existence. The perpetuation of ignorance is a most grievous form of oppression; it reinforces the many walls of prejudice that stand as barriers to the realization of the oneness of humankind, at once the goal and operating principle of Bahá'u'lláh's Revelation. Access to knowledge is the right of every human being, and participation in its generation, application and diffusion a responsibility that all must shoulder in the great enterprise of building a prosperous world civilization—each individual according to his or her talents and abilities. Justice demands universal participation.

21

Ultimately, the power to transform the world is effected by love, love originating from the relationship with the divine, love ablaze among members of a community, love extended without restriction to every human being. This divine love, ignited by the Word of God, is disseminated by enkindled souls through intimate conversations that create new susceptibilities in human hearts, open minds to moral persuasion, and loosen the hold of biased norms and social systems so that they can gradually take on a new form in keeping with the requirements of humanity's age of maturity. You are channels for this divine love; let it flow through you to all who cross your path. Infuse it into every neighborhood and social space in which you move to build capacity to canalize the society-building power of Bahá'u'lláh's Revelation. There can be no rest until the destined outcome is achieved.

Gossip & Backbiting

BAHÁ'U'LLÁH

1

Breathe not the sins of others so long as thou art thyself a sinner. Shouldst thou transgress this command, accursed wouldst thou be, and to this I bear witness.

2

B ackbiting quencheth the light of the heart,
and extinguisheth the life of the soul.

3

Verily I say, the tongue is for mentioning what is good, defile it not with unseemly talk. God hath forgiven what is past. Henceforward everyone should utter that which is meet and seemly, and should refrain from slander, abuse and whatever causeth sadness in men. Lofty is the station of man!

4

Beware lest ye give ear to the words of those from whom the foul smell of malice and envy can be discerned; pay no heed to them, and stand ye for righteousness.

'ABDU'L-BAHÁ

5

How blessed are these aims, especially the prevention of backbiting! I hope that you may become confirmed therein, because the worst human quality and the most great sin is backbiting; more especially when it emanates from the tongues of the believers of God. If some means were devised so that the doors of backbiting could be shut eternally and each one of the believers of God unsealed his tongue in the praise of the other, then the teachings of His Holiness Bahá'u'lláh would be spread, the hearts illuminated, the spirits glorified and the human world would attain to everlasting felicity.

6

If any individual should speak ill of one who is absent, it is incumbent on his hearers, in a spiritual and friendly manner, to stop him, and say in effect: would this detraction serve any useful purpose? Would it please the Blessed Beauty, contribute to the lasting honor of the friends, promote the holy Faith, support the covenant, or be of any possible benefit to any soul? No, never! On the contrary, it would make the dust to settle so thickly on the heart that the ears would hear no more, and the eyes would no longer behold the light of truth.

7

If any soul speak ill of an absent one, the only result will clearly be this: he will dampen the zeal of the friends and tend to make them indifferent. For backbiting is divisive, it is the leading cause among the friends of a disposition to withdraw.

8

One must see in every human being only that which is worthy of praise. When this is done, one can be a friend to the whole human race. If, however, we look at people from the standpoint of their faults, then being a friend to them is a formidable task. . . .

Thus is it incumbent upon us, when we direct our gaze toward other people, to see where they excel, not where they fail.

SHOGHI EFFENDI

9

In order to achieve this cordial unity one of the first essentials insisted on by Bahá'u'lláh and 'Abdu'l-Bahá is that we resist the natural tendency to let our attention dwell on the faults and failings of others rather than on our own. Each of us is responsible for one life only, and that is our own. Each of us is immeasurably far from being "perfect as our heavenly Father is perfect" and the task of perfecting our own life and character is one that requires all our attention, our will-power and energy. If we allow our attention and energy to be taken up in efforts to keep others right and remedy their faults, we are wasting precious time. . . .

On no subject are the Bahá'í teachings more emphatic than on the necessity to abstain from faultfinding and backbiting while being ever eager to discover and root out our own faults and overcome our own failings.

10

We must never dwell too much on the attitudes and feelings of our fellow-believers towards us. What is most important is to foster love and harmony and ignore any rebuffs we may receive; in this way the weakness of human nature and the peculiarity or attitude of any particular person is not magnified, but pales into insignificance in comparison with our joint service to the Faith we all love.

11

If we are better, if we show love, patience, and understanding of the weakness of others, if we seek to never criticize but rather encourage, others will do likewise, and we can really help the Cause through our example and spiritual strength.

12

He will also pray that the believers may, for the sake of God, draw close to each other and not permit each other's short-comings to be a source of disunity and consequently a means of depriving thirsty souls of this life-giving Message! The world is full of evil and dark forces and the friends must not permit these forces to get hold of them by thinking and feeling negatively towards each other.

THE UNIVERSAL HOUSE
OF JUSTICE

13

The environment sought is, at the most fundamental level, one of love and support, in which the believers, all endeavoring to achieve the Bahá'í standard in their personal conduct, show patience and respect to each other and, when needed, receive wise counsel and ready assistance. Gossip and backbiting have no place in the Bahá'í community; nor do judgmental attitudes and self-righteousness.

14

The friends should understand that they should not only cease backbiting and gossiping, but should cease listening to others who fall into this sin. Ignoring gossip and slander is a positive, constructive and healing action helpful to the community, the gossiper and to the persons slandered.

Service

BAHÁ'U'LLÁH

1

That one indeed is a man who, today, dedicateth himself to the service of the entire human race. The Great Being saith: Blessed and happy is he that ariseth to promote the best interests of the peoples and kindreds of the earth. In another passage He hath proclaimed: It is not for him to pride himself who loveth his own country, but rather for him who loveth the whole world. The earth is but one country, and mankind its citizens.

2

This Wronged One testifieth that the purpose for which mortal men have, from utter nothingness, stepped into the realm of being, is that they may work for the betterment of the world and live together in concord and harmony.

3

Wert thou to consider this world, and realize how fleeting are the things that pertain unto it, thou wouldst choose to tread no path except the path of service to the Cause of thy Lord. None would have the power to deter thee from celebrating His praise, though all men should arise to oppose thee.

Go thou straight on and persevere in His service. Say: O people! The Day, promised unto you in all the Scriptures, is now come. Fear ye God, and withhold not yourselves from recognizing the One Who is the Object of your creation. Hasten ye unto Him. Better is this for you than the world and all that is therein. Would that ye could perceive it!

4

They who are possessed of riches, however, must have the utmost regard for the poor, for great is the honor destined by God for those poor who are steadfast in patience. By My life! There is no honor, except what God may please to bestow, that can compare to this honor. Great is the blessedness awaiting the poor that endure patiently and conceal their sufferings, and well is it with the rich who bestow their riches on the needy and prefer them before themselves.

5

O Son of Man! Bestow My wealth upon My poor, that in heaven thou mayest draw from stores of unfading splendor and treasures of imperishable glory.

6

To give and to be generous are attributes of Mine; well is it with him that adorneth himself with My virtues.

7

Say: The appointed Day is come. This is the Springtime of benevolent deeds, were ye of them that comprehend. Strive ye with all your might, O people, that ye may bring forth that which will truly profit you in the worlds of your Lord, the All-Glorious, the All-Praised.

8

Charity is pleasing and praiseworthy in the sight of God and is regarded as a prince among goodly deeds. . . . Blessed is he who preferreth his brother before himself. Verily, such a man is reckoned, by virtue of the Will of God, the All-Knowing, the All-Wise, with the people of Bahá who dwell in the Crimson Ark.

‘ABDU’L-BAHÁ

9

Service to the friends is service to the Kingdom of God, and consideration shown to the poor is one of the greatest teachings of God.

10

In the love of God you must become distinguished from all else. You must become distinguished for loving humanity, for unity and accord, for love and justice. In brief, you must become distinguished in all the virtues of the human world—for faithfulness and sincerity, for justice and fidelity, for firmness and steadfastness, for philanthropic deeds and service to the human world, for love toward every human being, for unity and accord with all people, for removing prejudices and promoting international peace. Finally, you must become distinguished for heavenly illumination and for acquiring the bestowals of God. I desire this distinction for you. This must be the point of distinction among you.

11

We know that to help the poor and to be merciful is good and pleases God, but knowledge alone does not feed the starving man, nor can the poor be warmed by knowledge or words in the bitter winter; we must give the practical help of Loving-kindness.

12

And the honor and distinction of the individual consist in this, that he among all the world's multitudes should become a source of social good. Is any larger bounty conceivable than this, that an individual, looking within himself, should find that by the confirming grace of God he has become the cause of peace and well-being, of happiness and advantage to his fellow men? No, by the one true God, there is no greater bliss, no more complete delight.

13

God has given us eyes, that we may look about us at the world, and lay hold of whatsoever will further civilization and the arts of living. He has given us ears, that we may hear and profit by the wisdom of scholars and philosophers and arise to promote and practice it. Senses and faculties have been bestowed upon us, to be devoted to the service of the general good; so that we, distinguished above all other forms of life for perceptiveness and reason, should labor at all times and along all lines, whether the occasion be great or small, ordinary or extraordinary, until all mankind are safely gathered into the impregnable stronghold of knowledge. We should continually be establishing new bases for human happiness and creating and promoting new instrumentalities toward this end. How excellent, how honorable is man if he arises to fulfill his responsibilities; how wretched and contemptible, if he shuts his eyes to the welfare of society and wastes his precious life in pursuing his own selfish interests and personal advantages. Supreme happiness is man's, and he beholds the signs of God in the world and in the human soul, if he urges on the steed of high endeavor in the arena of civilization and justice.

14

I desire that your hearts may be directed to the Kingdom of God, that your intentions may be pure and sincere, your purposes turned toward altruistic accomplishment unmindful of your own welfare; nay, rather, may all your intentions center in the welfare of humanity, and may you seek to sacrifice yourselves in the pathway of devotion to mankind.

15

In the Bahá'í Cause arts, sciences and all crafts are (counted as) worship. The man who makes a piece of notepaper to the best of his ability, conscientiously, concentrating all his forces on perfecting it, is giving praise to God. Briefly, all effort and exertion put forth by man from the fullness of his heart is worship, if it is prompted by the highest motives and the will to do service to humanity. This is worship: to serve mankind and to minister to the needs of the people. Service is prayer. A physician ministering to the sick, gently, tenderly, free from prejudice and believing in the solidarity of the human race, he is giving praise.

SHOGHI EFFENDI

16

We must be like the fountain or spring that is continually emptying itself of all that it has and is continually being refilled from an invisible source. To be continually giving out for the good of our fellows undeterred by the fear of poverty and reliant on the unfailing bounty of the Source of all wealth and all good—this is the secret of right living.

THE UNIVERSAL HOUSE
OF JUSTICE

17

Service to others is the way. Let it be your watchword, 'Abdu'l-Bahá being your exemplar. Like Him, you can find practical ways of serving your fellow citizens. Strive to work hand in hand, shoulder to shoulder, with your fellow citizens in your efforts to promote the common good.

This surely is a time for the gallantry of illumined souls.

18

. . . understanding the implications of the Revelation, both in terms of individual growth and social progress, increases manifold when study and service are joined and carried out concurrently. There, in the field of service, knowledge is tested, questions arise out of practice, and new levels of understanding are achieved.

19

Learning as a mode of operation requires that all assume a posture of humility, a condition in which one becomes forgetful of self, placing complete trust in God, reliant on His all-sustaining power and confident in His unfailing assistance, knowing that He, and He alone, can change the gnat into an eagle, the drop into a boundless sea. And in such a state souls labor together ceaselessly, delighting not so much in their own accomplishments but in the progress and services of others. So it is that their thoughts are centered at all times on helping one another scale the heights of service to His Cause and soar in the heaven of His knowledge.

20

For is it not love for God that burns away all veils of estrangement and division and binds hearts together in perfect unity? Is it not His love that spurs you on in the field of service and enables you to see in every soul the capacity to know Him and to worship Him? Are you not galvanized by the knowledge that His Manifestation gladly endured a life of suffering out of His love for humanity?

21

. . . work performed in the spirit of service to one's fellow human beings is a form of prayer, a means of worshipping God. Translating ideals such as these into reality, effecting a transformation at the level of the individual and laying the foundations of suitable social structures, is no small task, to be sure. Yet the Bahá'í community is dedicated to the long-term process of learning that this task entails, an enterprise in which increasing numbers from all walks of life, from every human group, are invited to take part.

22

To follow a path of service, whatever form one's activity assumes, requires faith and tenacity. In this connection, the benefit of walking that path in the company of others is immense. Loving fellowship, mutual encouragement, and willingness to learn together are natural properties of any group of youth sincerely striving for the same ends, and should also characterize those essential relationships that bind together the components of society.

23

Challenged by self-serving power, pursue the acquisition of knowledge; in the face of fanaticism, build unity, and combat prejudices of all kinds; in response to enmity and hatred, offer love and show mercy and compassion; rather than surrendering to consumerism, live a selfless life of service and use your resources for the betterment of the world. Consort in fellowship and work with all who strive for these noble aims.

24

But in our concern for such immediate obvious calls upon our succor we must not allow ourselves to forget the continuing, appalling burden of suffering under which millions of human beings are always groaning—a burden which they have borne for century upon century and which it is the Mission of Bahá'u'lláh to lift at last. The principal cause of this suffering, which one can witness wherever one turns, is the corruption of human morals and the prevalence of prejudice, suspicion, hatred, untrustworthiness, selfishness and tyranny among men. It is not merely material well-being that people need. What they desperately need is to know how to live their lives—they need to know who they are, to what purpose they exist, and how they should act towards one another; and, once they know the answers to these questions they need to be helped to gradually apply these answers to everyday behavior. It is to the solution of this basic problem of mankind that the greater part of all our energy and resources should be directed.

Society, Economics,
and the Environment

BAHÁ'U'LLÁH

1

Every age hath its own problem, and every soul its particular aspiration. The remedy the world needeth in its present-day afflictions can never be the same as that which a subsequent age may require. Be anxiously concerned with the needs of the age ye live in, and center your deliberations on its exigencies and requirements.

2

All men have been created to carry forward an ever-advancing civilization.

3

. . . is not the object of every Revelation to effect a transformation in the whole character of mankind, a transformation that shall manifest itself, both outwardly and inwardly, that shall affect both its inner life and external conditions?

'ABDU'L-BAHÁ

4

Every human being has the right to live; they have a right to rest, and to a certain amount of well-being. As a rich man is able to live in his palace surrounded by luxury and the greatest comfort, so should a poor man be able to have the necessaries of life. Nobody should die of hunger; everybody should have sufficient clothing; one man should not live in excess while another has no possible means of existence.

Let us try with all the strength we have to bring about happier conditions, so that no single soul may be destitute.

5

Certainly, some being enormously rich and others lamentably poor, an organization is necessary to control and improve this state of affairs. It is important to limit riches, as it is also of importance to limit poverty. Either extreme is not good. To be seated in the mean is most desirable. If it be right for a capitalist to possess a large fortune, it is equally just that his workman should have a sufficient means of existence.

A financier with colossal wealth should not exist whilst near him is a poor man in dire necessity. When we see poverty allowed to reach a condition of starvation it is a sure sign that somewhere we shall find tyranny. Men must bestir themselves in this matter, and no longer delay in altering conditions which bring the misery of grinding poverty to a very large number of the people. The rich must give of their abundance, they must soften their hearts and cultivate a compassionate intelligence, taking thought for those sad ones who are suffering from lack of the very necessities of life.

There must be special laws made, dealing with these extremes of riches and of want. The members of the Government should consider the laws of God when they are framing plans for the ruling of the people. The general rights of mankind must be guarded and preserved.

6

Wealth is praiseworthy in the highest degree, if it is acquired by an individual's own efforts and the grace of God, in commerce, agriculture, art and industry, and if it be expended for philanthropic purposes. Above all, if a judicious and resourceful individual should initiate measures which would universally enrich the masses of the people, there could be no undertaking greater than this, and it would rank in the sight of God as the supreme achievement, for such a benefactor would supply the needs and insure the comfort and well-being of a great multitude. Wealth is most commendable, provided the entire population is wealthy. If, however, a few have inordinate riches while the rest are impoverished, and no fruit or benefit accrues from that wealth, then it is only a liability to its possessor. If, on the other hand, it is expended for the promotion of knowledge, the founding of elementary and other schools, the encouragement of art and industry, the training of orphans and the poor—in brief, if it is dedicated to the welfare of society—its possessor will stand out before

God and man as the most excellent of all who live on earth and will be accounted as one of the people of paradise.

7

Regarding reciprocity and cooperation, each member of the body politic should live in the utmost comfort and welfare because each individual member of humanity is a member of the body politic, and if one member is in distress or is afflicted with some disease, all the other members must necessarily suffer. For example, a member of the human organism is the eye. If the eye should be affected, that affliction would affect the whole nervous system. Hence, if a member of the body politic becomes afflicted, in reality, from the standpoint of sympathetic connection, all will share that affliction since this [one afflicted] is a member of the group of members, a part of the whole. Is it possible for one member or part to be in distress and the other members to be at ease? It is impossible! Hence, God has desired that in the body politic of humanity each one shall enjoy perfect welfare and comfort.

SHOGHI EFFENDI

8

As we view the world around us, we are compelled to observe the manifold evidences of that universal fermentation which, in every continent of the globe and in every department of human life, be it religious, social, economic or political, is purging and reshaping humanity in anticipation of the Day when the wholeness of the human race will have been recognized and its unity established. A twofold process, however, can be distinguished, each tending, in its own way and with an accelerated momentum, to bring to a climax the forces that are transforming the face of our planet. The first is essentially an integrating process, while the second is fundamentally disruptive. The former, as it steadily evolves, unfolds a System which may well serve as a pattern for that world polity towards which a strangely-disordered world is continually advancing; while the latter, as its disintegrating influence deepens, tends to tear down, with increasing violence, the antiquated barriers that seek to block humanity's progress towards its destined goal. The constructive process stands associated with the nascent Faith of Bahá'u'lláh, and is the harbinger of the New World Order that Faith must erelong establish. The destructive forces that characterize the other should be identified with a civilization that has refused to answer to the expectation of a new age, and is consequently falling into chaos and decline.

A titanic, a spiritual struggle, unparalleled in its magnitude yet unspeakably glorious in its ultimate consequences, is being waged as a result of these opposing tendencies, in this age of transition through which the organized community of the followers of Bahá'u'lláh and mankind as a whole are passing.

9

It is becoming evident that the world is not yet through with its labour, the New Age not yet fully born, real Peace not yet right around the corner. We must have no illusions about how much depends on us and our success or failure. All humanity is disturbed and suffering and confused; we cannot expect to not be disturbed and not to suffer—but we don't have to be confused. On the contrary, confidence and assurance, hope and optimism are our prerogative.

10

The believers, to better understand their own internal condition, should realize that the forces of darkness in the World are so prevalent and strong that their morbid and turbulent influence is felt by all. They should therefore consciously strive to be more loving, more united, more dedicated and prayerful than ever before, in order to fight against the atmosphere of present day society which is unloving, disunited, careless of right and wrong, and heedless of God.

11

When such a crisis sweeps over the world no person should hope to remain intact. We belong to an organic unit and when one part of the organism suffers all the rest of the body will feel its consequence. This is in fact the reason why Bahá'u'lláh calls our attention to the unity of mankind. But as Bahá'ís we should not let such hardship weaken our hope in the future. . . .

THE UNIVERSAL HOUSE
OF JUSTICE

12

They [Bahá'ís] are called upon to become increasingly involved in the life of society, benefiting from its educational programs, excelling in its trades and professions, learning to employ well its tools, and applying themselves to the advancement of its arts and sciences. At the same time, they are never to lose sight of the aim of the Faith to effect a transformation of society, remolding its institutions and processes, on a scale never before witnessed. To this end, they must remain acutely aware of the inadequacies of current modes of thinking and doing—this, without feeling the least degree of superiority, without assuming an air of secrecy or aloofness, and without adopting an unnecessarily critical stance towards society.

13

Today, in this age of transition, as humanity struggles to attain its collective maturity, such relationships—nay, the very conception of the individual, of social institutions, and of the community—continue to be assailed by crises too numerous to count. The worldwide crisis of authority provides proof enough. So grievous have been its abuses, and so deep the suspicion and resentment it now arouses, that the world is becoming increasingly ungovernable—a situation made all the more perilous by the weakening of community ties.

Every follower of Bahá'u'lláh knows well that the purpose of His Revelation is to bring into being a new creation. . . . At a fundamental level these relationships are characterized by cooperation and reciprocity, manifestations of the interconnectedness that governs the universe.

14

The purpose of every Manifestation of God is to effect a transformation in both the inner life and external conditions of humanity. And this transformation naturally occurs as a growing body of people, united by the divine precepts, collectively seeks to develop spiritual capacities to contribute to a process of societal change.

15

The light of the Revelation is destined to illumine every sphere of endeavor; in each, the relationships that sustain society are to be recast; in each, the world seeks examples of how human beings should be to one another. We offer for your consideration, given its conspicuous part in generating the ferment in which so many people have recently been embroiled, the economic life of humanity, where injustice is tolerated with indifference and disproportionate gain is regarded as the emblem of success. So deeply entrenched are such pernicious attitudes that it is hard to imagine how any one individual can alone alter the prevailing standards by which the relationships in this domain are governed. Nevertheless, there are certainly practices a Bahá'í would eschew, such as dishonesty in one's transactions or the economic exploitation of others. Faithful adherence to the divine admonitions demands there be no contradiction between one's economic conduct and one's beliefs as a Bahá'í. By applying in one's life those principles of the Faith that relate to fairness and equity, a single soul can uphold a standard far above the low threshold by which the world measures itself. Humanity is weary for want of a pattern of life to which to aspire; we look to you to foster communities whose ways will give hope to the world.

16

The welfare of any segment of humanity is inextricably bound up with the welfare of the whole. Humanity's collective life suffers when any one group thinks of its own well-being in isolation from that of its neighbours or pursues economic gain without regard for how the natural environment, which provides sustenance for all, is affected. A stubborn obstruction, then, stands in the way of meaningful social progress: time and again, avarice and self-interest prevail at the expense of the common good. Unconscionable quantities of wealth are being amassed, and the instability this creates is made worse by how income and opportunity are spread so unevenly both between nations and within nations. But it need not be so. However much such conditions are the outcome of history, they do not have to define the future, and even if current approaches to economic life satisfied humanity's stage of adolescence, they are certainly inadequate for its dawning age of maturity. There is no justification for continuing to perpetuate structures, rules, and systems that manifestly fail to serve the interests of all peoples. The teachings of the Faith leave no room for doubt: there is an inherent moral dimension to the generation, distribution, and utilization of wealth and resources.

17

Humanity would be best and most effectively served by setting aside partisan disputation, pursuing united action that is informed by the best available scientific evidence and grounded in spiritual principles, and thoughtfully revising action in the light of experience. The incessant focus on generating and magnifying points of difference rather than building upon points of agreement leads to exaggeration that fuels anger and confusion, thereby diminishing the will and capacity to act on matters of vital concern.

18

On the matter of climate change and other vital issues with profound implications for the common good, Bahá'ís have to avoid being drawn into the all too common tendencies evident in contemporary discourse to delineate sharp dichotomies, become ensnared in contests for power, and engage in intractable debate that obstructs the search for viable solutions to the world's problems.

19

Bahá'ís are encouraged to see in the revolutionary changes taking place in every sphere of life the interaction of two fundamental processes. One is destructive in nature, while the other is integrative; both serve to carry humanity, each in its own way, along the path leading towards its full maturity. The operation of the former is everywhere apparent—in the vicissitudes that have afflicted time-honored institutions, in the impotence of leaders at all levels to mend the fractures appearing in the structure of society, in the dismantling of social norms that have long held in check unseemly passions, and in the despondency and indifference exhibited not only by individuals but also by entire societies that have lost any vital sense of purpose. Though devastating in their effects, the forces of disintegration tend to sweep away barriers that block humanity's progress, opening space for the process of integration to draw diverse groups together and disclosing new opportunities for cooperation and collaboration. Bahá'ís, of course, strive to align themselves, individually and collectively, with forces associated with the process of integration. . . .

20

The deepening environmental crisis, driven by a system that condones the pillage of natural resources to satisfy an insatiable thirst for more, suggests how entirely inadequate is the present conception of humanity's relationship with nature; the deterioration of the home environment, with the accompanying rise in the systematic exploitation of women and children worldwide, makes clear how pervasive are the misbegotten notions that define relations within the family unit; the persistence of despotism, on the one hand, and the increasing disregard for authority, on the other, reveal how unsatisfactory to a maturing humanity is the current relationship between the individual and the institutions of society; the concentration of material wealth in the hands of a minority of the world's population gives an indication of how fundamentally ill-conceived are relationships among the many sectors of what is now an emerging global community. The principle of the oneness of humankind implies, then, an organic change in the very structure of society.

21

When so much of society invites passivity and apathy or, worse still, encourages behavior harmful to oneself and others, a conspicuous contrast is offered by those who are enhancing the capacity of a population to cultivate and sustain a spiritually enriching pattern of community life.

22

Passivity is bred by the forces of society today. A desire to be entertained is nurtured from childhood, with increasing efficiency, cultivating generations willing to be led by whoever proves skilful at appealing to superficial emotions. Even in many educational systems students are treated as though they were receptacles designed to receive information. That the Bahá'í world has succeeded in developing a culture which promotes a way of thinking, studying, and acting, in which all consider themselves as treading a common path of service—supporting one another and advancing together, respectful of the knowledge that each one possesses at any given moment and avoiding the tendency to divide the believers into categories such as deepened and uninformed—is an accomplishment of enormous proportions. And therein lie the dynamics of an irrepressible movement.

23

Today the world is assailed by an array of destructive forces. Materialism, rooted in the West, has now spread to every corner of the planet, breeding, in the name of a strong global economy and human welfare, a culture of consumerism. It skilfully and ingeniously promotes a habit of consumption that seeks to satisfy the basest and most selfish desires, while encouraging the expenditure of wealth so as to prolong and exacerbate social conflict. How vain and foolish a worldview! And meanwhile, a rising tide of fundamentalism, bringing with it an exceedingly narrow understanding of religion and spirituality, continues to gather strength, threatening to engulf humanity in rigid dogmatism. In its most extreme form, it conditions the resolution of the problems of the world upon the occurrence of events derived from illogical and superstitious notions. It professes to uphold virtue yet, in practice, perpetuates oppression and greed. Among the deplorable results of the operation of such forces are a deepening confusion on the part of young people everywhere, a sense of hopelessness in the ranks of those who would drive progress, and the emergence of a myriad social maladies.

The key to resolving these social ills rests in the hands of a youthful generation convinced of the nobility of human beings; eagerly seeking a deeper understanding of the true purpose of existence; able to distinguish between divine religion and mere superstition; clear in the view of science and religion as two independent yet complementary systems of knowledge that propel human progress; conscious of and drawn to the beauty and power of unity in diversity; secure in the knowledge that real glory is to be found in service to one's country and to the peoples of the world; and mindful that the acquisition of wealth is praiseworthy only insofar as it is attained through just means and expended for benevolent purposes, for the promotion of knowledge and toward the common good.

NOTES

Unity & Cooperation

BAHÁ'U'LLÁH

1. *Gleanings from the Writings of Bahá'u'lláh,* no. 146.1.
2. Ibid., no. 111.1.
3. *Tablets of Bahá'u'lláh,* no. 7.20.
4. *The Summons of the Lord of Hosts,* p. 68.
5. Epistle to the Son of the Wolf, p. 14.
6. The Hidden Words, no. 68 from the Arabic.

'ABDU'L-BAHÁ

7. *The Promulgation of Universal Peace,* pp. 478–79.
8. *Paris Talks,* no. 9.21.
9. *The Promulgation of Universal Peace,* p. 128.
10. *Selections from the Writings of 'Abdu'l-Bahá,* no. 15.6.
11. Ibid., no. 7.2.
12. Ibid., no. 1.3.

13. Ibid., no. 8.8.

14. *The Promulgation of Universal Peace*, pp. 215–16.

15. Ibid., pp. 241–42.

SHOGHI EFFENDI

16. *The World Order of Bahá'u'lláh*, p. 202.

17. *The Promised Day Is Come*, ¶286.

18. From a letter dated 13 May 1945 written on behalf of Shoghi Effendi to the National Spiritual Assembly of Australia and New Zealand, in *The Compilation of Compilations, Vol. II*, no. 1307.

THE UNIVERSAL HOUSE OF JUSTICE

19. To the Bahá'ís of the World, 25 November 2020. Available at https://www.bahai.org/library/authoritative-texts/the-universal-house-of-justice/messages/20201125_001/1#300076438.

20. To the Bahá'ís of Iran, 2 March 2013, in *Framework for Action*, no. 23.6.

Consultation, Action, Reflection, and Study

BAHÁ'U'LLÁH

1. *Tablets of Bahá'u'lláh*, no. 11.15.

2. From a Tablet, translated from the Persian, in *The Compilation of Compilations, Vol I*, no. 168.

3. *Tablets of Bahá'u'lláh*, no. 11.15.

4. From a Tablet, translated from the Arabic, in *The Compilation of Compilations, Vol I,* no. 167.

5. From a Tablet, translated from the Persian, in *The Compilation of Compilations, Vol I,* no. 170.

'ABDU'L-BAHÁ

6. From a Tablet, translated from the Persian, in *The Compilation of Compilations, Vol. I,* no. 179.

7. Ibid., no. 180.

8. Ibid., no. 185.

9. *Selections from the Writings of 'Abdu'l-Bahá,* no. 43.1.

10. Ibid., no. 44.1.

11. *The Promulgation of Universal Peace,* pp. 99–100.

12. *Selections from the Writings of 'Abdu'l-Bahá,* no. 39.2.

13. Quoted in the Guardian's letter, dated February 15, 1922 to the National Spiritual Assembly of Persia, in *Lights of Guidance,* no. 580.

SHOGHI EFFENDI

14. *Bahá'í Administration,* pp. 63–64.

15. Ibid., p. 79.

16. From a letter written on behalf of Shoghi Effendi to an individual believer, 30 August 1933, in *The Compilation of Compilations, Vol. I,* no. 196.

17. From a letter dated 30 June 1949 written on behalf of Shoghi Effendi to the National Spiritual Assembly of Germany and Austria, in *The Compilation of Compilations, Vol. II*, no. 1383.

THE UNIVERSAL HOUSE OF JUSTICE
18. To the Bahá'ís of the World, Riḍván 2008, in *Framework for Action*, no. 10.1.
19. To the Conference of the Continental Boards of Counsellors, 29 December 2015, *Framework for Action*, no. 35.14.
20. To the Bahá'ís of the United States, July 22 2020. Available at https://www.bahai.org/library/authoritative-texts/the-universal-house-of-justice/messages/20200722_001/1#870410257.
21. To the Bahá'ís of Iran, 2 March 2013, in *Framework for Action*, no. 23.10.
22. To the Bahá'ís of the World, Riḍván 2014. https://universalhouseofjustice.bahai.org/ridvan-messages/20140421_001.

Elimination of Prejudices

BAHÁ'U'LLÁH
1. *Gleanings from the Writings of Bahá'u'lláh*, no. 156.1.
2. In *The Compilation of Compilations, Vol. II*, no. 2093.
3. *Tablets of Bahá'u'lláh*, no. 7.33.

'ABDU'L-BAHÁ

4. *The Promulgation of Universal Peace*, p. 640.
5. *Selections from the Writings of 'Abdu'l-Bahá*, no. 202.3.
6. *The Promulgation of Universal Peace*, p. 94.
7. Ibid., p. 53.
8. Ibid., p. 401.
9. *Paris Talks*, no. 40.19–21.
10. Ibid., no. 41.7–8.
11. *The Promulgation of Universal Peace*, p. 103.
12. *Selections from the Writings of 'Abdu'l-Bahá*, no. 227.18.
13. *The Promulgation of Universal Peace*, p. 106.

SHOGHI EFFENDI

14. *The Advent of Divine Justice*, ¶59.
15. On behalf of Shoghi Effendi to individual believers, 3/25/49, Microfilm Collection of the Original Letters of Shoghi Effendi, National Bahá'í Archives, Wilmette, IL.
16. *The Advent of Divine Justice*, ¶51.

THE UNIVERSAL HOUSE OF JUSTICE

17. To the Bahá'ís of the United States, 22 July 2020. Available at https://www.bahai.org/library/authoritative-texts/the-universal-house-of-justice/messages/20200722_001/1#870410257.
18. Letter written on behalf of the Universal House of Justice, dated May 31, 1992, to an individual believer.

19. *The Promise of World Peace*, p. 8.
20. To the Bahá'ís of the World, Riḍván 2010, in *Framework for Action*, no. 14.29.
21. To the Bahá'ís of the United States, 22 July 2020. Available at https://www.bahai.org/library/authoritative-texts/the-universal-house-of-justice/messages/20200722_001/1#870410258.

Gossip & Backbiting

BAHÁ'U'LLÁH

1. The Hidden Words, Arabic no. 27.
2. The Kitáb-i-Íqán, ¶214.
3. *Tablets of Bahá'u'lláh*, no. 15.2.
4. *The Summons of the Lord of Hosts*, p. 172.

'ABDU'L-BAHÁ

5. Tablet to Dr. M. G. Skinner, August 12, 1913, in *Lights of Guidance*, no. 312.
6. *Selections from the Writings of 'Abdu'l-Bahá*, no. 193.8.
7. Ibid., no. 193.8.
8. Ibid., no. 144.2, no. 144.6.

SHOGHI EFFENDI

9. Letter dated 12 May 1925 to an individual believer, in *The Compilation of Compilations, Vol. II*, no. 1272.

10. Letter dated 19 September 1948 to an individual believer, in *Lights of Guidance,* no. 397.
11. Quoted in letter written on behalf Universal House of Justice dated August 13, 1980, in *Lights of Guidance,* no. 309.
12. From a letter written on behalf of Shoghi Effendi to an individual believer, January 27, 1945, in *Lights of Guidance,* no. 394.

UNIVERSAL HOUSE OF JUSTICE
13. To the National Spiritual Assembly of the Bahá'ís of Denmark, 23 April 2013, in *Framework for Action,* no. 52.4.
14. Letter from the Universal House of Justice, dated September 21, 1965, to a National Spiritual Assembly.

Service

BAHÁ'U'LLÁH
1. *Gleanings from the Writings of Bahá'u'lláh,* no. 117.1
2. From a Tablet, translated from the Persian, in *The Compilation of Compilations, Vol II,* no. 2032.
3. *Gleanings from the Writings of Bahá'u'lláh,* no. 144.2–3.
4. Ibid., no. 100.4.
5. The Hidden Words, Arabic no. 57.

6. Ibid., Persian no. 49.
7. In *The Compilation of Compilations, Vol. I*, no. 1123.
8. *Tablets of Bahá'u'lláh*, no. 6.36.

'ABDU'L-BAHÁ

9. *Selections from the Writings of 'Abdu'l-Bahá*, no. 11.1.
10. *The Promulgation of Universal Peace*, pp. 265–66.
11. *'Abdu'l-Bahá in London*, p. 61.
12. *The Secret of Divine Civilization*, ¶5.
13. Ibid., ¶6.
14. *The Promulgation of Universal Peace*, p. 74.
15. *Paris Talks*, no. 55.1.

SHOGHI EFFENDI

16. *Principles of Bahá'í Administration*, p. 20.

THE UNIVERSAL HOUSE OF JUSTICE

17. To the Bahá'í students deprived of access to higher education in Iran, 9 September 2007, in *Framework for Action*, no. 7.12–13.
18. To the Bahá'ís of the World, Riḍván 2010, in *Framework for Action*, no. 14.9.
19. Ibid., no. 14.20.
20. Ibid., no. 14.33.
21. To the Bahá'ís of Iran, 2 March 2013, in *Framework for Action*, no. 23.9.

22. To the participants in the forthcoming 114 youth conferences throughout the world, 1 July 2013, in *Framework for Action*, no. 27.5.

23. To the Bahá'ís of Iran, 1 October 2014, in *Framework for Action*, no. 33.7.

24. From a letter written on behalf of the Universal House of Justice to the National Spiritual Assembly of Italy, November 19, 1974, in *Messages of the Universal House of Justice 1963–1986*, no. 151.5.

Society, Economics, and the Environment

BAHÁ'U'LLÁH

1. *Gleanings from the Writings of Bahá'u'lláh*, no. 106.1.

2. Ibid., no. 109.2.

3. The Kitáb-i-Íqán, ¶270.

'ABDU'L-BAHÁ

4. *Paris Talks*, no. 40.23–24.

5. Ibid., no. 46.10–12.

6. *The Secret of Divine Civilization*, ¶46.

7. *The Promulgation of Universal Peace*, pp. 435–36.

SHOGHI EFFENDI

8. *The World Order of Bahá'u'lláh*, p. 170.

9. *Unfolding Destiny*, p. 225.

10. From a letter written on behalf of Shoghi Effendi to the National Spiritual Assembly of the United States and Canada, 20 March 1946, in *Lights of Guidance,* no. 1346.

11. From a letter written on behalf of Shoghi Effendi to a Bahá'í family, April 14, 1932, in *Lights of Guidance,* no. 446.

THE UNIVERSAL HOUSE OF JUSTICE

12. To the Conference of the Continental Boards of Counsellors, 28 December 2010, in *Framework for Action,* no. 16.36.

13. Ibid., no. 16.40–41.

14. To the Bahá'ís of the World, Riḍván 2012, in *Framework for Action,* no. 21.3.

15. Ibid., no. 21.7.

16. To the Bahá'ís of the World, 1 March 2017. Available at https://universalhouseofjustice.bahai. org/involvement-life-society/20170301_001.

17. Letter dated 29 November 2017 to three individuals. Available at https://www.bahai.org/library/ authoritative-texts/the-universal-house-of-jus- tice/messages/20171129_001/1#831044059.

18. Ibid.

19. To the Bahá'ís of Iran, 2 March 2013, in *Framework for Action,* no. 23.4.

20. Ibid.

21. To the participants in the forthcoming 114 youth conferences throughout the world, 1 July 2013, in *Framework for Action,* no. 27.6.

22. To the Bahá'ís of the World, Riḍván 2010, in *Framework for Action,* no. 14.10.
23. Letter dated 2 April 2010 to the Believers in the Cradle of the Faith. Available at https://www.bahai.org/library/authoritative-texts/the-universal-house-of-justice/messages/20100402_001/1#378503622.

BIBLIOGRAPHY

Works of Bahá'u'lláh

Epistle to the Son of the Wolf. New ed. Translated by Shoghi Effendi. 1st ps ed. Wilmette, IL: Bahá'í Publishing Trust, 1988.

Gleanings from the Writings of Bahá'u'lláh. Translated by Shoghi Effendi. Wilmette, IL: Bahá'í Publishing, 2005.

The Hidden Words. Translated by Shoghi Effendi. Wilmette, IL: Bahá'í Publishing, 2002.

The Kitáb-i-Íqán: The Book of Certitude. Translated by Shoghi Effendi. Wilmette, IL: Bahá'í Publishing, 2003.

The Summons of the Lord of Hosts: Tablets of Bahá'u'lláh. Wilmette, IL: Bahá'í Publishing, 2006.

Tablets of Bahá'u'lláh revealed after the Kitáb-i-Aqdas. Compiled by the Research Department of the Universal House of Justice. Translated by Habib Taherzadeh et al. Wilmette, IL: Bahá'í Publishing Trust, 1988.

Works of 'Abdu'l-Bahá

'Abdu'l-Bahá in London: Addresses &Notes of Conver-sations. London: Bahá'í Publishing Trust, 1987.

Paris Talks: Addresses Given By 'Abdu'l-Bahá in Paris in 1911. Wilmette, IL: Bahá'í Publishing, 2011.

Promulgation of Universal Peace: Talks Delivered by 'Abdu'l-Bahá during His Visit to the United States and Canada in 1912. Compiled by Howard MacNutt. Wilmette, IL: Bahá'í Publishing, 2012.

The Secret of Divine Civilization. Translated by Marzieh Gail and Ali-Kuli Khan. Wilmette, IL: Bahá'í Publishing, 2007.

Selections from the Writings of 'Abdu'l-Bahá. Compiled by the Research Department of the Universal House of Justice. Translated by a Committee at the Bahá'í World Center and Marzieh Gail. Wilmette, IL: Bahá'í Publishing, 2010.

Works of Shoghi Effendi

The Advent of Divine Justice. 1st pocket-size ed. Wilmette, IL: Bahá'í Publishing Trust, 1990.

Bahá'í Administration. Wilmette, IL: Bahá'í Publishing Trust, 1998.

The Promised Day is Come. Wilmette, IL: Bahá'í Publishing Trust, 1993.

Unfolding Destiny: The Messages from the Guardian of the Bahá'í Faith to the Bahá'í Community of the British Isles. London: Bahá'í Publishing Trust of the United Kingdom, 1981.

The World Order of Bahá'u'lláh: Selected Letters. New ed. Wilmette, IL: Bahá'í Publishing Trust, 1991.

Works of the Universal House of Justice

Framework for Action: Selected Messages of the Universal House of Justice and Supplementary Material, 2006–2016. West Palm Beach, FL: Palabra Publications, 2017.

Messages from the Universal House of Justice, 1963–1986: The Third Epoch of the Formative Age. Compiled by Geoffry Marks. Wilmette, IL: Bahá'í Publishing Trust, 1996.

The Promise of World Peace: A Statement from the Universal House of Justice. October, 1985.

Bahá'í Compilations

The Compilation of Compilations: Prepared by the Universal House of Justice, 1963–1990. 2 vols. Australia: Bahá'í Publications Australia, 1991.

Lights of Guidance: A Bahá'í Reference File. Compiled by Helen Hornby. New ed. New Dehli, India: Bahá'í Publishing Trust, 1994.

Principles of Bahá'í Administration. Compiled by the National Spiritual Assembly of the Bahá'ís of the United Kingdom. London: Bahá'í Publishing Trust, 1973.